JUBILEE

ANHINGA PRESS

JUBILEE

ROXANE BETH JOHNSON

2005 PHILIP LEVINE PRIZE FOR POETRY

Selected by Philip Levine

ANHINGA PRESS, 2006
TALLAHASSEE, FLORIDA

Cover art: *Above the Meadow* (oil and collage on panel)
            by John McCormick
Author photo: Derron Santin
Cover design, book design, and production: C. L. Knight
Typesetting: Jill Ihasz
Type Styles: titles and text set in Schneidler Light

Library of Congress Cataloging-in-Publication Data
Jubilee by Roxane Beth Johnson – First Edition
ISBN – 0-938078-92-5 (978-0-938078-92-0)
Library of Congress Cataloging Card Number – 2006929375

This publication is sponsored in part by a grant
from the Florida Department of State,
Division of Cultural Affairs, and the Florida Arts Council.

Anhinga Press Inc. is a nonprofit corporation dedicated wholly to the
publication and appreciation of fine poetry and other literary genres.

For personal orders, catalogs and information write to:
Anhinga Press
P.O. Box 10595
Tallahassee, Florida 32302
Web site: www.anhinga.org
E-mail: info@anhinga.org

Published in the United States
by Anhinga Press
Tallahassee, Florida
First Edition, 2006

For my brother, Perry

CONTENTS

ACKNOWLEDGMENTS

Thanks to the editors of the following publications where some of the poems in this book appeared: *ZYZZYVA, American Poet, Parthenon West Review, The Noe Valley Voice, The Throwback,* and *Nocturnes (Re)View.*

"Weeknight Services" was short-listed for a Pushcart Prize and "Mulatto" won the AWP Intro Writer's Award in Poetry. "Hell" was printed as a special edition, letter set broadside from The SF Center for the Book in 2005.

Many thanks to the following individuals for their support, reading and comments: Toni Mirosevich, Dan Langton, Denise Caruso, Truong Tran, Allison Busch, Lory Bedikian, Lydia Wills, Chad Sweeney, and the editors at Anhinga Press. Thanks again and again to Pony Smith for his close reading and re-reading of this manuscript.

A special thanks to Paul Hoover, who was tremendously helpful and inspiring, and to Philip Levine for choosing my book.

NOTES

The structure of "Mulatto" is loosely based on Linh Dinh's "The Most Beautiful Word."

The title "Off in the darkness houses move restlessly from dream to dream" is a misquote of a misquote from Albert Goldbarth's poem, "Off in the darkness hourses moved restlessly."

JUBILEE

STORE FRONT CHURCH

SUNDAY NIGHT SERVICES

Daddy's afro wide as a rain cloud. Aunties in glossy white boots,
twirling like dervishes to the beat. Rinsed in music, we were
singing, *I'm a soldier, in the army of the Lord*. Repeat. There was a
laying on of hands; anointing the head with oil. *Jesus be the only
thing you need,* was what we sang. Paper fans slapped, fluttered in
the rigid August heat. A cousin got the Holy Ghost and then he
spoke in tongues. White stuff came out of his mouth, down his
chin. Cousin prayed faster, clapped harder. *That's the devil leaving
his soul,* Momma said. I had to look instead of pray. That was
how I got a beating. The preacher screamed, *Close your eyes and
pray. Say thank you Jesus! Say it again.* I said it again and again.
We beat the tambourine. That was how we praised His holy
name. Preacher liked to hit me. That was how it was. We sang,
Help yourself to the blood of Jesus. The piano's orange music sparkled.
I had to listen. Jesus be my sweet librarian, my quiet consolation
— this is what I learned to pray.

BURDEN OF LIGHT

Our church was full of whores and gamblers. The preacher taught me to pray by banging my palms together like two fish she was trying to kill. The preacher taught me to pray the way a lantern protects fire from air — by a false, caged force. Our church shook with holy-rollers and the preacher was my grandmother. Our church had scriptures written on the walls. One said Jesus said, *My yoke is easy and my burden is light.* I thought of Jesus eating a fried egg, over-easy, the yolk bright like flame. Our church was full of sinners crying, *Jesus, Jesus, Jesus.* I was possessed by mistakes and my prayers were wrong. The preacher taught me how to navigate darkness, how to travel with a burden of light.

WEEKNIGHT SERVICES

The organ's flare-hued opera hummed loud
in the small church alcove above the bar
with its bumpy music. Our voices wound
up being too small to drown it out by far.
We sung of Jesus' blood with a tambourine,
one drum, twenty voices, paper fans, bells —
while the thump-thump of bass through the ceiling
made rhythm that silenced our fears of hell,
demons, white folks, Catholics, death's certain flood.
But the music — blood of Jesus, God bless
the child I was then — that music: *The blood,*
we sang would wash us white as snow. *Blessed*
assurance, Jesus is mine, Oh ... what fears.
When I hear those drums, my heart is in my ears.

CALL SONG

This is a poem about white people coming into our church. They come to hear the music, don't care about salvation. They come to hear the choir sing, sit in the back smelling like perfume. They are looking for the darkness, a sound that makes them feel something. They don't know what, we say, *It's shame*. They come to hear music that sounds bigger, wider than theirs. They don't know why but their parents owned us so they believe it's theirs. This is a poem about white people coming into our church and they say I am beautiful, I look almost white. They don't care about salvation. They come to hear the choir sing. This is a poem about the choir singing off-key and the preacher getting mad. This is a poem about the preacher getting mad when the white people say I am pretty, I look almost white and the music is divine, clapping their hands. This is a poem about the preacher shaking her cane at them, waving it above their heads like Jesus in the temple, beating away the thieves. This is a poem about the preacher who spat rage like a mouthful of blood. This is a poem about white people who came to our church. To hear the music. Had to hurry, leave but with a tale to tell, *How crazy black people are! Did you see the preacher hit that beautiful child?*

ARTIFACT FOUND BURIED UNDER RIBS

This is the sea where I was baptized at five. Watch the preacher hold my hand as we lumber chest high into the lavish water. See my thin, white nightgown billow out like a jellyfish. This is where she does not let go of me, but see how she places her hand so gentle on my head, a true prayer. Look at that sky, watch it as I pinch my nose and take a deep breath. Close your eyes tight as you can: that is the last sparked darkness I see before being put under. See the preacher lower me into the ocean's white sizzle. Be buried in its deafening roar.

COMPANY

A traveling preacher comes to our house for coffee. He takes it hot and black, pours it on the saucer and sips it like that. He is the fattest man I have ever seen. We sit with him at the kitchen table. We watch him drink his coffee from a saucer. He asks, *Have you got anything to eat, Sista Johnson?* My mother says, *I've got some chili and bread.* He says, *Sounds good!* While she cooks, the preacher and my father talk about Jesus. The chili smells of too-salty meat and onions. The bread is warm and yeasty in the oven. *You right,* my father says to everything the preacher says. The preacher doesn't talk to me. When my mother puts the plate in front of him, he places the bread on the table. Just like that! Nothing under it, not even a napkin. He asks for butter. Momma gets the butter dish and a knife, and before she can set it down, he takes it from her. Uses the knife to scrape the half-cube into his chili. My mother stands behind him with her hands open for a moment, her fingers curved around the memory of something she lost.

THE TRAVELING PREACHER AT TEN

Migration of applause settled in the cavity
of your ear, like birds on a roof.
Mama's brassieres drip drying on the shower rod.
Radio music minnowing through rooms like fear
humming, always in the background of things.

No school, God taught you what you know.
How to *get up, get up now* and drive daddy
home from Lou's Bar on Third,
how to *keep out the way* when half-sober
he pointed the rifle straight at her.

Stockings were up that night, dangling ghosted
and parched in the iced bathroom air.
How she unfolded her heavy black arms
like wings or resolutions, and looked down
like Jesus on the fans, hanging from his hinges.

All those black and white fans being fanned in the church
were pigeons just let out of a coop, flying nowhere,
just circling and swaying, leashed and fretted.

He carries her old pink garter in his pocket
to preach, not for luck — for luck is for the sinner
taking his chances — but for a blessing.
And also, the smell — mercuried and everlasting —
of the spent cartridge echoing in the house.

TAMBOURINE

Tambourines make the dark air go silver with sound. Black hands shake and bang them like crashing down plates. The sound is a snow storm's falling if a snow storm's sound were not a howling. Tambourine stings my palm. I hit it hard like banging a door with my flattened hand because I am tired of knocking. I shake it like mother shakes me, shakes me, and then I am the tambourine — my bones jangling like a circle of cymbals.

PRELUDE

A bum walks into our storefront church. His coat is torn and he smells like whiskey. He sits on the back pew and lets his head hang down, like the ducks in Chinatown. He will die here quiet as a bird alive flies. Quiet as Jesus slipping out of the tomb.

DEATH TAKES WHAT'S MINE

When a homeless man comes into church to die, don't look at the faces when his breathing gets heavy. Heavy like that bird you saw in the doorway. It couldn't fly. His eyes are like that bird's — unmoving. The others' eyes are low, like half moons — delicate and soft. Don't hear the tenderness in their voices as they sing *Blessed Assurance* and your father holds the dying man's hand. How might it feel to have your hand held in that way; the heat of daddy's gold ring pressing into your palm? When the hobo dies, when they say he's gone home to Jesus, when their voices rise up singing, let it be unbearable in you. Let the agony of that old drunk getting your love slice you open like daddy gutting a fish. Go ahead and say it. Say, *Old wino, who cares!* Now, everyone will look at you the way you are used to. Eyes pointed in rage, mouths turned down like you fed them bitterness that was supposed to be sweet.

CHOCOLATE CIGARETTES

Praise the Lord, the preacher yells. *Praise the Lord*, everyone yells.
I don't say. Praise Aunt Carol, stepping out to smoke. Standing
still and looking into the dark, holding fire and swirling white
soot. Aunt Carol puts it in her mouth, closes her eyes as she
breathes smoke in, puckers it out. A calyx of shapes. I wish she
were mine. She comes back and whispers, *Couldn't take it in here
for one more second*. Her breath tingles on my face, a hot breeze of
mint and fire smoke. Praise to Aunt Carol. I ask for a cigarette.
Nasty habit, they say. Praise Aunt Carol. I wish she were mine.
One day she gives me a box of chocolate cigarettes. I eat them
all the way home.

AUNT CONNIE LEADS
THE YOUTH BAPTISMAL PROCESSION

Let them think it will take place in a big bathtub. Cleaned
with bleach and glistening like spilled salt. Rent the AME
Baptist Church's baptismal font. Lead the children down a
brownly lit corridor. Put them in big white choir robes. Say,
Fold your hands, close your eyes, think of Jesus dying cross-
like for your sins. Hold your breath. Baptize them in the blood
of Jesus. Wash like snow. Rise up spitting water. Hair wetted
and napping up. Hurry, put some oil on that scalp before it
dries out! Say, Thank you Jesus! Here is some strawberry Kool-
Aid and coconut cake. Don't spill on the carpet. Shut your
mouth when you chew. Lord, keep them on this long road of
life. Washed in the blood, white as snow.

A CHILD'S BLUES

This is my mother. She's the devil. The preacher says so.
                                        See mother cry.
This is my father, the preacher's favorite son. He says, *Shut-up.*
                                        Quiet now.
These are bees. They shouldn't be here. Mother's thoughts
                                        are bees in a jar.

These are my other grandparents. They live in a big house
                                        with cherry trees out back.
Mother asks if we can live with them. Without Daddy.
                                        Please say yes.
This is Granddad. Hear him say, *You made your bed, lie in it.*
                                        Quiet now. Hear bees inside.

This is me. I say, *Devils aren't so bad. There's devil's food cake
                                        and deviled eggs.*
This is me saying, *Momma! Listen ... those are good things to eat.*
                                        Momma! Listen.
Mother looks at me. Bees drop dead in the jar. *Shut up,*
                                        she says. Quiet now.

NEW YEAR'S EVE
ALL-NIGHT PRAYER SERVICE, 1973

Hours came and left like drinkers from the bar next door. Some of us prayed with our eyes open. The moon faced another continent.

One of us, my Grandfather Deke, sang, *Swing Low, Sweet Chariot* as bar music pounded. He taught us perseverance amid distraction, even if you did look like a fool.

The preacher turned the lights off. I was afraid of the dark; this meant living in a worst-case scenario for an indeterminate period of time. As with all bad times, it didn't last.

For those of us who had hope, the preacher yelling, *Get behind me, Satan! Get behind me Satan* — made us quiet, listening for diminishing footsteps, a crumpling of the dark.

Some grew tired. We slept and dreamed of being small animals chased in the snow. At the very last moment, a hole in the ground received us.

At dawn, someone shouted, *Hallelujah!* We stood up, our aching knees still concentrated toward carpet.

Some of us wondered what we were there for. Some might say: we were on the lookout, in search of God. Now I know that's all it was: brilliance was our prey.

MIRACLE HEALING

The preacher says, *Jesus will heal your weary and burdened body.*
You don't say? She says, *Oh, yes.* Cavities of poor people filled
with heavenly gold, spines straightened like wrinkles ironed from
a shirt, madness soothed by God's breath. Don't make me laugh.
I laugh. It becomes a sickness. I am sick with the devil's double
spirit — laughter. She says I'd be better off dead than laugh in
the House of the Lord.

The House of the Lord smells of Jesus' wounds; we've all got our
fist of stones. The preacher anoints my head with oil. Her fat
finger circles grease on my brow. She tells me, *Jesus will heal you,
make you right again, chile.* You don't say? I laugh right in her
face, throw my head back like an opera singer as she hits that
last wild note before driving in the knife.

ALPHABET DECONSTRUCTION

The preacher says if I keep laughing in church, I will get hit by a bus. And die. She is the New Jesus, so she knows these things. Momma and daddy whisper-talk in the car on the way home, repeating the words quiet, like a call song. *Hit by a bus,* daddy says. *That's crazy,* momma says. Listen, I have the secret now. I can hear under words. Hear seas rushing in and back, spoons and forks jangling on the table, the oven opening with a creak and whine, revealing unbaked things. Under words are cars rushing over wet roads. My parents drive away from me. I wave goodbye. I stand alone on the wet street. Laughter crowns me. Cars rush toward me. When the bus hits me, I am flat as a pancake, my blood glittering around me like a sky full of stars.

GRANDFATHER DEKE'S BOX
I'm gonna lay down my burdens, down by the riverside ...

We buried you with room for your heart that weighs an ounce, dried of its liquid need. Here, there is no place for the interconnecting rooms and neighborhoods; instead rise and lightly wander new lands with your small box of self. Walking as memory weightless hovers like your wide white afro — a star's nimbus. The family tribe asks for bone dust to give to a new one. Don't. Keep the body's remnants: the untraveled places, untouched shoulders of women and friends, the grasping and being pulled away. There is the river. Keep all sorrow to yourself. Put it in the box. It is light as a pencil, jangly as a nail in a jar. You may need it to build yourself back together one day. You just might do that, anyway. Shelled of skin, your life is tiny as a seed. There is not even an ounce of flesh.

SUFFERING SPECULATION

Imagine Aunt Connie's body — a car packed with locusts,
                                        windows shut.
Imagine death under her bed — wrenching out the nerves
                                        of her body.
Imagine her nourishment — syrup drip of morphine
                                        slowing traffic.

Let me write this story of how she accompanied herself
                                        to her dying.
Let me think of her ovaries as spoiled peaches, a crush
                                        of flies feasting.
Let me see her workers driving tractors — mowing down
                                        every cell in sight.

Speculate on her suffering — stare at the ringed fist that will
                                        punch her bloody.
Complete the following sentences — this is how she lived
                                        before the diagnosis:
This is why she decided to refuse treatment and let her body
                                        be eaten:

Remember my Aunt liked to fry up collard greens with bacon
                                        and butter.
Imagine saying what those bitter roadside weeds tasted like
                                        in her mouth.

AUNT CONNIE

She is thirty-five when we bury her, a gorgeous orange rotted through. Cold coats the sky like frost on car windows. Her funeral is called a "home-going." Everyone wears white. The choir sings, the preacher moans the gospel of the risen Christ. My father cries.

Back at her house, we chew on chicken bones and scrape our plates. Mother takes a lilac dress from things the husband sets out. *Girl, you'll look good in that color,* Aunt Connie says, flashes her skinny smile. *Wrong size,* mother says back to the empty room. She decides to keep it after all. Some everlasting beauty is always needed — like wax fruit or a photograph: a memory too small to wear.

TELLING MYSELF HOW IT ALL ENDED

We never go back. We leave as if running away in the middle of the night, mother yanking us out of warm beds and driving us over the precipice. Our car floats midair, pre-ocean. The sky that holds us is polished onyx and smells like fog. We journey for nights and nights. The day does not arrive for years, having scattered behind us like a shooting star. The life we lived becomes memory and is hazy, spilled salt. We move fast, our bodies in the car blur behind us.

COMMUNION OF SAINTS

There was the church. It was white and square, the inside of a shoebox. There were six rows of splintery pews. The bathroom in the back dripped water that tasted like rust. You had to hold your index finger up as you walked past the podium to go to the bathroom. If the preacher didn't want you to go, she told you to sit down no matter how bad you had to pee. You know Churchgranny. She was the preacher. My grandmother. You know my mother — she was the devil. There was my father. There was the pew where I sat next to my mother. Those were the people. From here I can see everyone. There is Aunt Leah. She wears earrings that look like bells. You don't know this now, but Churchgranny will kill her when she is thirty. There is Uncle Jeffrey, Uncle Sidney. One will end up living forever in the back of a van; the other will die in jail. There are others, the Holy Ghost. Scent of hair oil. If you need to pee, you should try to hold it rather than walk during the preaching. There is my father now. He is singing a song. *Give me that old time religion.* … I get up to go pee now. He looks at me and nods. As if to say yes. He holds cruelty close to him, as close as hands clapping. Here are his hands. He has given it to me twice. Both times, my mother laughed.

JUBILEE

Potluck Easter lunch in our store-front church. Dead Aunt Connie blows stale breath on a steaming soup bowl. Dead Grandfather Deke chews his sweet potato pie. Nostalgia. Other faces, pale as pewter. This old hunger follows me like the moon. Jesus is blessing baskets that expand with fish like hundreds of brown birds lighting on bare trees. On this Easter, we flock to apparitions of food, put already eaten cake and cold-cuts, bread with butter, into mouths sheer as jellyfish. The body of Christ moves among us, a breeze in the cool of the day. Incandescent. Our dark fingers twitch and flutter, like coils of soot. Negatives. A borrowed kindness fills the room like furniture to be gathered up and moved. Migration. We eat with our hands as the ancient plates dissolve like snow. Hallelujah. The walls are mounds of salt. We stand in piles of salt, our ashes. I've got to throw this all over my back. I've been watching this old movie so long it will crumble like Communion on my tongue. We sing into the wind. Jubilee.

THE HOLY GHOST

What passed between us then? A show of hands, an exchange of faces blue as rain. The Holy Ghost. What was it that held us? A gasp — at birds dashing into windows and falling stunned into the grass. A shared mumbling. Who were we then but voices linked like storm clouds gathering. We danced around, spoke in tongues. Liars. What do we hold now? Bible's gold edges tarnished by our dark fingers. Sing it: *Sweet holy spirit, sweet heavenly dove ...* Holy Ghost appears in dreams without a tongue, her mouth a silent vowel, tender as Mary humming as she washed Jesus' feet.

CHERRY ORCHARD

STUDY OF GRANDFATHER TONY
IN HIS ORCHARD AT DAWN

He feels alive. There is mildew on his mind. Blue sky underlined
with a stripe of rust. The cherry trees are black as burnt wicks in
this light. Today his son will go to Viet Nam. His fingers touch
trunks. Squeezes palm on a limb, feels the texture of leaves.
Paper crumpling. A bizarre jungle green. He feels alive. There is
opera on his mind. *La Traviata*. There is water on his mind, DDT,
a string of pearls for his wife. He holds hoses. Hears the ripening
of the fruit. It's the sound of doors slowly closing. The figs are
yearning for his mouth. With coffee they are fine. All is stark
and concentrated as a baby's first scream. His son will be in
Viet Nam tomorrow at this time. He wants to scream that he is
alive. Today his wife will go to the bank with the last payment.
There are crows on his mind.

ONLY YOU

Grandfather Tony, it's you I remember. When I look toward home, you stand by the cherry trees. The blossoms drizzle over your body. No, it is not like that, not like looking back. It is an inheritance; your old reading lamp on my desk pouring dusty yellow light. You in your box in the earth. The color of your bones, that same yellow light. No, it is not that. It is not the thought of you now or then. Is it the continuous angel that appears in the shape of dreams, shifting you to another, a lion, then you again? It's you deadheading roses at dusk, ankle high in brown petals and knuckled branches. You whistling an aria, working until night was a shroud. Your voice was too loud, your cheek whiskers sharp. You nodding off in the old rocking chair having forgotten your name. It's you walking along the roof, sweeping off the soggy winter leaves. You coming out of the church in a tuxedo black as a smudge of coal, Grandma's gown a sheath of frost. Yes. That's you, smiling at me in that clownish white and red stripped dress I wore to my first midnight mass. Not looking at my bright white tights and toes hanging over the edge of my sandals. You said I looked like the Fourth of July.

STUDY OF GRANDFATHER WORKING
IN HIS GARDEN AT NOON

His body's best memory is choreography of leaf grasp and
deadheading, stomping down the mulch. Feeding plants their
lexicon of dirt. Language digests and betrays him. Lemon trees
admire him, flashing their fragrant yellow eyes. Peels one, gives
rind and the soft, flaring flesh to his teeth. Sweet to his accepting
tongue. A dense, worked life has come to this. He is a bucket of
crocus bulbs; plain as a barn with a museum inside. In the east,
bad weather is coming. California is the place to be for this body
that can direct earth even in sleep. It is never winter here.

HOLY WATER

Perry and I go with Grandma Ella to her church, St. John of the Cross. The preacher (*priest*, Grandma corrects me later) preaches quietly, not like Churchgranny at all, who screams and shakes her big, brown Bible the way Momma shakes out a dust rag. On the way out, Grandma puts her fingers in a stone bowl of water, touches her forehead and her shoulders. Perry looks inside the bowl of water, leans over and laps like a cat. People laugh. Grandma Ella takes Perry's hand and says, *Shame on you! That's Holy water!* We can't stop laughing. *What did it taste like,* I ask Perry in the car on the way home. *Kinda fruity.*

BIRDS

Grandma Ella hangs a mirror on the kitchen window to keep birds from flying into it. Still, one zooms in, drops like a swatted fly on the patio. A brisk thud and crack marks the moment. *Stupid bird!* Grandma yells. *Stupid bird!* I yell. We look at the flotsam body, I see the black beaded eye. She scoops it up with a spatula and paper bag. Poor birds. They think they are just flying through. They don't know that clarity will kill them. Wings folded in as they fall like hands pressed together in prayer.

MULATTO

Grandma is washing me white. I am the color of hot sand in the bleached sea light. I am a stain on the porcelain, persistent as tea. Stay in the shade. Don't say she was the only one. Cousins opposite say: you too white. I am a night-blooming flower being pried open in the morning. My skin a curtain for a cage of bones, a blackbird coop. My heart is crusty bread, hardening. Hardening. This way, I feed my own fluttering. Under shade, the day looks like evening and I cannot bear the darkness. Don't say, I can't stand to be touched. Say, I stare into the sun to burn off the soiled hands that print my body with bloody ink. Don't say, *Mulatto*. Say, I am the horse in Oz turning different colors, each prance brightening flesh. A curiosity. Don't say, Bathwater spiraled down into the pipes. Say, I never did fade. Say, Skin holds the perseverance of my days. Folding, folding, the water continuously gathers, making wrinkles in a map.

LATER

Granddad is in the garden with a nozzle stuffed down a hole, the green hose fat and rigid with water, trying to flush out a gopher. I am six and horrified. Would the gopher swim out, dazed and gasping? Would he be spit out, his fur wetted to his body, his eyes looking sharp but dead? *Il Travatore* plays on the phonograph. Grandma in the kitchen says, *Granddad's gone to kill that lousy gopher! He's ruining my lilies.* She sits at her sewing machine, foot on peddle making it run and hum. When I dream this place years later, she's there mumbling, *Lilies, kill my lillies* and her needle plunges faster, deeper into invisible fabric — and Granddad, in his blue jean overalls, is tearing up the grass and lilies with his rusty hoe as hundreds of moths loosed from the mud are drawn right to his body all aflame.

OFF IN THE DARKNESS, HOUSES MOVE RESTLESSLY FROM DREAM TO DREAM
Misquote read somewhere

That old house arrives pure as tea having rinsed off its orchard and the crawling vines. Windows are asterisks. Egg beige walls smell like a book. Under a kitchen counter, a grocery bag is damp with grease. This old house loves no one but me, takes me in like a goldfish swallowed whole. Glittery voice in stucco and pipe, breathes in the wind and out a company of silverfish. Your armpits grow potted flowers and old dresses float in your secret places. House, you press down on me like a lover — feet on grass, your body on mine.

352 HELMSLEY DRIVE

MOTHER AND FATHER, 1965

Don't look at them. My mother and father in a school yard. She's a blinding white diamond. Don't watch as she takes the ring, puts it on. He is black as a candle wick. Words clog their throats like fruit stuck to its pit. Stop them now, my mother and father. Stop them rushing towards earth's more unreasonable affections. Look at me. Me there, hovering like dust kicked up by bare feet running. Look at me — waiting, wanting to be born.

ROLLER-SKATING

Roller-skating backward on hot, bumpy
asphalt. Summer. Hearing the sparkling disco
beat of the roller rink in my head
like a monotonous chant as I fly
past the handsome boy's candy-apple
red hotrod, past the fluffy behinds of dogs.
Being backward is familiar as thorns on a rose,
dizzy thrill of not seeing the holes
in the road, the faces of those who aren't friends.
Lawns slide by. Thin trees push away
from me, the sidewalk reels in like a clothes line.
The horizon grows smaller, goes farther.
There go the twisted knots of mother's house
like stains coming loose in the wash.

WHAT I DO

Eat cereal. Read the back of the box over and over. Put on my red velvet jumper with white heart shaped buttons. Walk to the bus, pick up discarded cigarette butts and pretend to smoke.

Get on the bus. Girls yell, *Wire head, ugly black skin*. Take a window seat, under the radio speaker. Look for cats hunting in the fields.

Go to class. Stay in at recess. Steal chewing gum, plastic green monkeys and cookies from desks. Eat in bathroom stalls. Pure white light pours in.

Try to get a bloody nose by punching myself in the same bathroom after lunch.

The teacher passes around pictures of herself pregnant. *You were fat!* I yell. Everyone laughs. I lap it like licking honey from a spoon. *I was pregnant, what's your excuse?* Everyone laughs. I swallow stones.

Grow tired in the afternoons, droop like a sunflower in the lengthening light.

Get on the bus. Girls yell, *Brillo-head! Zebra!* Sit in an aisle seat. *Your father's a nigger!* I say, *No, he's a fireman*. Laughter all around. Pinch myself shut like squeezing soap from a sponge.

Walk home. Sometimes find an unsmoked cigarette in the gravel along the curb — long, white, new. Put it to my lips, pull it away and hold it aloft, movie-star-like, all the way home.

Sometimes mom plays the piano and I hear it coming up the sidewalk.

Stand in hallway, watch the sun soak up walls and carpet, listen to the piano — someone's lost cigarette in my hand.

SPIDER MAN

I am standing outside her bedroom door, watching Mother whip my brother with my father's dung colored belt. His screams shoot lightning through my bones. I stand in the door's crack of light, looking with one shaky eye. There is music in the house. Trumpets are screaming; the piano keys are made of tin. The belt makes a meaty sound on his skin like slapping heavy steaks over and over on a dish of herbs. Mother yells between blows. Her words are rusty bike chains sticking. My brother claws and jumps for the walls, a crazy dog trying to bust out of a cage. In our room later, through swollen lips, my brother says he thought he was Spider Man — full of red slashes — so, why couldn't he climb the wall and get away?

PORTRAIT OF MYSELF IN A NEW DRESS

I would sometimes watch my mother lay out a new dress on the carpet. This was always at night when my father had eaten burgers and rice, or chicken and rice, and was waiting for the ball scores or Johnny Carson, staring at the twinkling screen the way headlights point ahead, livid and constant. She'd pin the thin paper pattern on the material, usually a printed cotton or, once, a glossy lime green velveteen, careful to get the bias right, pins sticking out from her lips. She made so many dresses for herself and me, always in the off-hours when the tub had been rinsed and the frying pans scraped of their sticky fat or left to soak overnight. Always cutting fabric — the sharp hissing sound the scissors made like matches struck over and over — always the motor of the sewing machine making its little threaded tracks over flowers and polka-dots or, one time, lime green velveteen. My father glaring ahead deeper and deeper into the night. Me on the school bus in the morning in a just-made dress or skirt, stiff with newness and the sweet smell of fried onions.

CHILDHOOD

I walk into the candy store and my father is chewing a gooey chocolate-toffee, the syruped almonds cracking between his teeth. This is years ago. His teeth are false because, as a child, his mother punched them out. I don't think about that being over, but of it being parallel. Equal. Balanced. Like music playing as we talk. This is what being born teaches me. My father chewing sweets and swallowing his teeth.

POP

I go to buy a cold drink and my Father's nine-year old ghost
follows me into the store, says,

I just wanted a cherry pop is all   got some money from caddying
for old white man Donovan gave me enough for a pop for me
and Jeffrey too   At O'Reilley's, I buy pop and we lean on our
bikes drinkin' it up   the sun skillet hot the air wavy hot   what
you pickinninies doin' cop says   Jeffrey says, Nothin', Sir   I
say nothin' meaning I keep my mouth shut look down they
think I'm dumb but I know   Jeffrey talks and they want to take
our bikes 'cause all niggers do nowadays is steal from good White
kids   Jeffrey holds on to the handlebars knuckles getting pink
and they kick him hard in the behind   he akimbos over with a
yelp like a kicked dog   so I let go stand to the side   keep
looking down they think I'm dumb   No   I just know not to
look   I don't want to dream their eyes.

ALARM

as told to me by my father

Lots of false alarms after 2 a.m. But, you never could tell. People take too many pills, shoot themselves after the Late Show. Sometimes a building really is burning. Smell of smoke as soon as you get outside the station. You get so you know. There was that 4:30 a.m. call from a mother. Young mother. Baby not moving. Eyes not blinking. Open eyes. *Possible false alarm,* dispatcher says. Me and Schwartze drive without talking because we know. Sometimes a fire is what you need. In the house, baby smell of lotion and soap. The baby's room is blasting with spirits. Schwartze opens the window. I know you've got to cover the body and when I do, the father cries. *This may be a false alarm,* the mother says.

MY FATHER EXPERIENCING LIGHT

I want to say something for my father as he ran at sunset. Look at those wine colored running shorts and new silver Adidas. Listen to all the neighborhood kids and me who yelled after him like he was a champ. How far did he run, how long? I want to say he ran within feverish shafts of yellow-red brilliance like that Morris Graves bird, his delicate mortality enduring in the burning light. When he came through on the other side, I want to say, he was no longer the same.

SELF-PORTRAIT AT TEN

A boarded-up house. Ransacked inside — broken glass and toppled tables, chairs overturned, books shaken for hidden money.

There are mouths in dreams full of gold teeth, chewing bread and meat. The body is hollow as flame and will burn down anything if pointed straight.

A bird flies in through the door, then flutters at the window. Although he is tiny, I am too afraid to help him escape.

I've made myself another house. I hum to fill its empty rooms. I fold in like saloon doors closing, then swinging out, keeping out thieves.

SATURDAY AFTERNOON, INTERIOR

What I keep of mother: the feel of hands as she pierced my ears
with needle, alcohol and ice.

Warm fingers like a loaf of baked bread, smooth with roughness
of hot water and bleach.

My own moist hand clenching my mouth, my head resting
on the table.

Silver needle to floss my lobe, her fingers knitting; a sharp tuck
of awful happiness sewn into flesh.

PIANO

Silence is voices — cancelled stamps on old envelopes, yellow as squash and stuck like blood on cloth.

Silence is round — littered with the shadows of my mother's fingers glistening over the piano keys like fog.

FIVE SCENES WITH MOTHER

She prayed for that last baby to die and when she saw its six-week old body like a bloody thumb in the toilet, said softly, *Thank you*.

There is a fire behind her ribs, bright as liquid glass before it is blown into something hard and useful.

She steps on a needle and howls. Her husband laughs. His laughter stops her, like a mouse caught in the thrilled teeth of a cat.

This is her cross. The devil lays his hands on her.

She escapes. Puts the children in the back of the old Thunderbird. At the Oregon coast, a craving makes her turn around. The sky shakes with birds.

SELF-PORTRAIT WITH CAKE, MATCH, AND LOVERS

The year I turn twelve, I've got nothing to show for myself but a tin box of bones which rattle and make me numb. I am misshapen as a can shot through with holes. Holes: I run into walls trying to stop the jangling in my brain. I listen to music so loud that the silence after is cold as my head in the freezer. I read halves of books. I skip school to eat cake. Eat cake and watch soaps. Mirrors are black when I look into them. Black as match tips, but lacking the possibility of flame. Flame: I consider setting the house on fire. I practice being beautiful in my head. I will be twelve for so long, until I am thirty, at least. Then, cake becomes the mouths of lovers, wet and sweet. Breathing rattles my bones. I am weary from falling like leaves.

DAYDREAM

My parents don't care. I could always hear them in the next room. My mother's soprano-high moans, like the intermittent creaking of a thin door left open on a windy night. My father's rhythmic grunts, the same grunt when trying to screw off the lid of a mayonnaise jar. His final *ahh*. The walls could not contain them. Sound came through like rats descending the stucco. Mother coming into the kitchen later, in a thin lace negligee though it was always afternoon. She'd open up the fridge, bend over to get a carton of milk, a piece of pie. She was contained at those times, as if alone in a daydream. Her dark pink nipples hanging down like two drops of blood squeezed from a finger.

HELL

HELL

To come back as yourself in the next life, ignore yourself in this one. To do this, fill your ears with stones. To come back as the person you hated most, save all their letters in old cigar boxes and eat them gingerly. Chew the words like cud. When you are reborn as that person, you will have plenty to say. To come back as a better person, piece memory together like a mosaic of broken tea cups, standing back for long moments to consider and revise your work. There will be something left over for next time. To bypass this hell completely, allow God to blow you hollow as a gourd.

THE PREACHER'S SUITE

*

EARLY DAYS

Drunk as bees, swerving in line for a table at Ming's Noodle Shop. They are thin as newly planted trees. Deke carries Viv's pocketbook. This is Fifth Street. Chinatown. 1941. They have been married six weeks. They want cheap noodles again for dinner, three or four beers each. Hot miso soup in chipped white bowls. Then, dance till eleven-thirty. Home. He rolls down her lace garters and dusty black stockings, her body leaning on his. *Girl, give me some love!* Too drunk again to consummate. Taller by a foot, she holds her liquor less. *I don't hafta pay noooo man no mind!* Did he keep on loving her? Was she never his flower, always his queen?

ONE MORNING WHILE HER HUSBAND STILL SLEEPS,

Viv lets go of her mind. Like her Mama wouldn't do that night thirty years back. Held her neck, made her see Daddy strung up a tree. Flames galloped him quick, plunging him through to cinder. The men wore white. They let go of the night, forced it wide with firelight. It can be like that, she knows, as easy as deciding it will be so. Viv lets go of her mind, puts it out like a bag of greasy rags to burn in a blazing box with trash, with junk you don't look at twice. This is how she does it, this is exactly the way: gets a hand mirror, holds her eyes steady to their own reflection like a glass under sun pointed toward grass will start a fire. Let the voices, let the devil have you. It's not hard to let go, your knuckles hurt bad from holding on so. There is a crack like summer thunder and everyone looks up. Her mind goes up in flames faster than a body might splashed with gasoline, lit with a match. There was the sound of insects when the violence ceased. She cannot let go of one thing, that scene — her mother early the next morning, gripping the hoe, raking up ashes and leaves.

TRANSFORMATION

It began with the Evangelist's hand on her head, moving it back and forth, holding it and shaking it as if it were a melon. His hand on her head, giving her the Holy Ghost. No, it began when he said, *Hello, might you spare a minute for the Lord?* A minute for the Lord, she wanted to kiss his mouth. It began when he took both her hands and raised them high, to *praise God!* and pelted her face with spit from screaming in tongues. *The spirit of the Lord descends like a dove.* No, it began when she wanted to kiss his mouth. It began when she had to give up drink, drink only of the Lord. *Say Hallelujah! Say Praise the Lord!* The words placed in her mouth like a hungry, wet tongue. It began two weeks before, when he was in town preaching out in a tent behind the trees. It began when she went to shout and holler, *Praise the Lord,* but really so he might save and hold her, shaking and shimming like so. Fool for the Lord, found a lover. One day, he'll return in glory to take what is his alone. Bride of Christ.

GHOST SUITE

*

OLD BROTHER

Lately a slave has been calling me. Calls, hangs up. Yells at me just as I fall asleep, yanking me back into waking with a shaky foil toned voice. Looks at me like I've done something wrong. His face is broken in places like a dilapidated puppet. Some nights he drips with urine and the scent of brine. Some nights he is fair as cold butter and calls himself Jacques. He says, *Dearest, if I press you right, I know you'll sing.* He won't tell me the lyrics. Like a mosquito trying to get in the window, he is put off by the glass. He's all broken up, bones brittle as old sea horses, left on the window sill to dry.

PORTRAIT OF MY GREAT-GREAT-GREAT GRANDPARENTS, SLAVES

Their lives grasp my skin around muscle and bone — like a father holding a child's small wrist. I dream their miscellany of thoughts: unwashed skin, dusk melting late behind fields. Smell of flour. Taste of dust. Standing behind the church for a photograph, there is Clea. There is Zebedee: sold! Now, the glance of Clea holding her daughter's hand — they watch Zebedee taken away. She sees this again and again. Like her tooth suddenly fallen out last week; her tongue constantly seeks that bloody hole.

LOVER'S SUITE

*

NICE WORK IF YOU CAN GET IT

My lovers come to kiss me goodbye each morning. Their eyes bright as gleaming bathtubs. Each morning they give me a pinch of tea for my cup. This one, in the corner scratching a scar on his neck, is a junkie. His bones await reassembly by the gods. This one translates from the Russian, each Christmas we share grape jelly on supermarket croissants. This one is a musician. He bought a plane seat for his guitar. There's the professor, a cabbie, a full-time drunk. Each one is here, surrounding me like songs. Turns out, their goodbyes were nothing; each one is always coming back. My favorite beloved, the last one always waiting for me at the door: the Kosher butcher who blessed each animal and called me doll. His hands are warm on my breasts, each finger coos like a dove.

OLD BOYFRIENDS

Like moles, they burrowed in the dark earth, carving labyrinths through the underground with the whites of their eyes for illumination. I closed my eyes and held their hands, trusting. Into walls they pressed me, lifted my shirt with furor, fumbling fast with the clasp on my bra. Twirled my nipples between glistening teeth and pushed their tongues into places I will never see. They smoked and kissed me with mouths full of fire. Liquor rose on their breath like the vapors more than one poet has breathed to die. That was a kind of love. Being naked with what was broken, pressing my body into theirs. Our shards fused like burning wax. There were others — my grandmother who preached to me of salvation and tribulation. I loved all my possessors; the first one who hollered in my ear as I prayed with eyes closed and forced me to look. What I saw was nothing but darkness, where I found everything I've got.

SUITE FOR MYSELF

*

OVERVIEW IN RED

Ten years in church. Five Sunday dresses. One red. The age I am when I learn to spark above my body like a bird in the house.

Eighteen years of love for my father. My words a valentine, a bottle of paprika Mother drops on the floor.

Fourteen years eating cherries from Grandfather's orchard. Their phantom taste longed for as a lost tongue, a missing limb.

Twelve years working in the city, circling red letter days. Trumpets blaring music in me; my therapist calls that crimson symphony: anxiety.

At twenty, I stop stuttering. My mouth gives up, moves its articulation to my hands. My hands become coals I press to my lips, become dumb with their burning.

First grade, I dream I am oiled and set on fire, running, fraying, lit as a torch. I chase my own smoke. From the start — a longing for what has passed.

At two years old: three minutes, maybe four — alone in a car with two dark uncles. Eyes wide like glistening fish. Three minutes, maybe four and my body is no longer my own. Thirty-five years looking for my ghost, ungraspable as hot, black tea.

JUNIOR

Under my skin, each ancestor lives. In my toes are the worries of the murdered house slave and an old Sicilian kneads her troubles like dough. Lodged in my bones are dry riverbeds of Grandfather Deke's Mississippi childhood. Cells float. Linked music gathered in my joints is my Aunts huddled together, singing gospel before they were twelve. Muscles cling to bone. In my ribs, great-grandmother brings up a length of rope, ties it to my hip-bones, pulls tight as a pinched nerve. Her death, a beating, is sketched on my face: hairline cracks echo various blows. There is fear in me, the sound of screams the color of sulfur. Chromosomes flare. My ancient cousin's death by lynching and flame cause my eyelashes to fall out.

AFFIRMATIONS SAID AT SEA

I am getting better:
nerves unknot like a choir of a single voice.

I am letting go:
my father was happiest when he fished;
came home with bloody sacks to freeze or fry.

I concentrate on beauty:
the others arrive at Mori Point ahead of me;
each body narrow as the letter *i*, backlit with sun.

I accept all sorrow:
driving fast, he flipped the top down like slamming back a drink.

I am beloved:
I have never seen a black peony;
the ocean is a soul hiding a body, letting birds float.

I am no longer afraid:
dying will be many of us traveling together.
A unity of sea birds running toward drier shore.

I am alive right now:
The water is gold and frilly.

I am learning to say goodbye:
How to end a story? *Change the subject, then slowly walk away.*

BLUES FOR ALMOST FORGOTTEN MUSIC

I am trying to remember the lyrics of old songs
$$\qquad\qquad\qquad\qquad\text{I've forgotten, mostly}$$
I am trying to remember one-hit wonders, hymns,
$$\qquad\qquad\qquad\text{and musicals like } West Side Story.$$
Singing over and over what I can recall, I hum remnants on
$$\qquad\qquad\qquad\qquad\text{buses and in the car.}$$

I am so often alone these days with echoes of these old songs
$$\qquad\qquad\qquad\qquad\text{and my ghosted lovers.}$$
I am so often alone that I can almost hear it, can almost feel
$$\qquad\qquad\qquad\qquad\text{the half-touch of others,}$$
can almost taste the licked clean spine of the melody I've lost.

I remember the records rubbed with static and the needle
$$\qquad\qquad\qquad\qquad\text{gathering dust.}$$
I remember the taste of a mouth so sudden and still cold from
$$\qquad\qquad\qquad\qquad\text{wintry gusts.}$$
It seemed incredible then — a favorite song, a love found.
$$\qquad\qquad\qquad\text{It wasn't, after all.}$$

Days later, while vacuuming, the lyrics come without thinking.
Days later, I think I see my old lover in a café but don't,
                              how pleasing
it was to think it was him, to finally sing that song.

This is the way of all amplitude: we need the brightness
                              to die some.
This is the way of love and music: it plays like a god and
                              then is done.
Do I feel better remembering, knowing for certain
                              what's gone?

TOAST

Thanks to you, Mother and Father, for giving me fear.
To you, love for trepidation and the piano
lending cadence to the drumroll of rain. To you,
the desperation I hunker under and call, *Sweetheart.*
(sweetheart, let me hold to you like an old black Bible).

From you, the world and its water boiling, memory constant
as light pulsing on off bright dark like Las Vegas
and always open just like that. You possess everyone
like water in the body. Stuffed me full
as a rusty lunch box, gave me all I need. Mother, Father

you hang around me languid as mothballed coats
that go limp with rain. From you, all that is hidden
and goes looking to hide, small animals fleeing fire.
To you, my world that fits into a nutshell:
give me my crown.

THE GREAT BY AND BY

One day I'll say: I'm glad my death is over.
I'm glad life will keep my body and slowly dissolve it,
darken and weaken it — tea leaves soaking in water.
I'll ask: why did I spend time thinking about death
while I was living? It's good I could never grasp it —
poppies can't see themselves on a California hillside.
Today I report: the weather still displays me in its museum.
My eternity — some kid with bloody knees playing anyway,
gravel and flesh creating a scar.

LETTER TO MY FORMER SELF

My family are birds now, balancing on wet black branches in the lime-leaved trees. I watch with the others for the hawk. Small breezes make us bounce, our bellies light with seed. Our one song prunes the silence. Brown, to blend with twigs, we are best in Autumn. We keep the wind company. We unhinge the clouds. We will stay this way. So, keep your swimming pools and radios, rice at weddings. Keep your costly love. All your talking like bright feathers lures the hunter. In dusk's steady burn-down, the sky lacquers black. No heavy luggage, just a brocade of stars at our backs.

ABOUT THE AUTHOR

Roxane Beth Johnson's poems have appeared in: *ZYZZYVA,
American Poet, Sentence, The Bitter Oleander, Chelsea, Parthenon West
Review,* and elsewhere. She has been a Pushcart Prize finalist and
was a recipient of an AWP Intro Writer's Award in Poetry. In
2006, she was awarded the Louis Untermeyer Scholarship in
Poetry by the Bread Loaf Writer's Conference. She lives and works
in San Francisco.

THE PHILIP LEVINE PRIZE FOR POETRY

2001
Breathing In, Breathing Out
Fleda Brown

2002
The Pyramids of Malpighi
Steve Gehrke

2005
Jubilee
Roxane Beth Johnson